GODEY'S FASHIONS
COLORING BOOK

Ming-Ju Sun

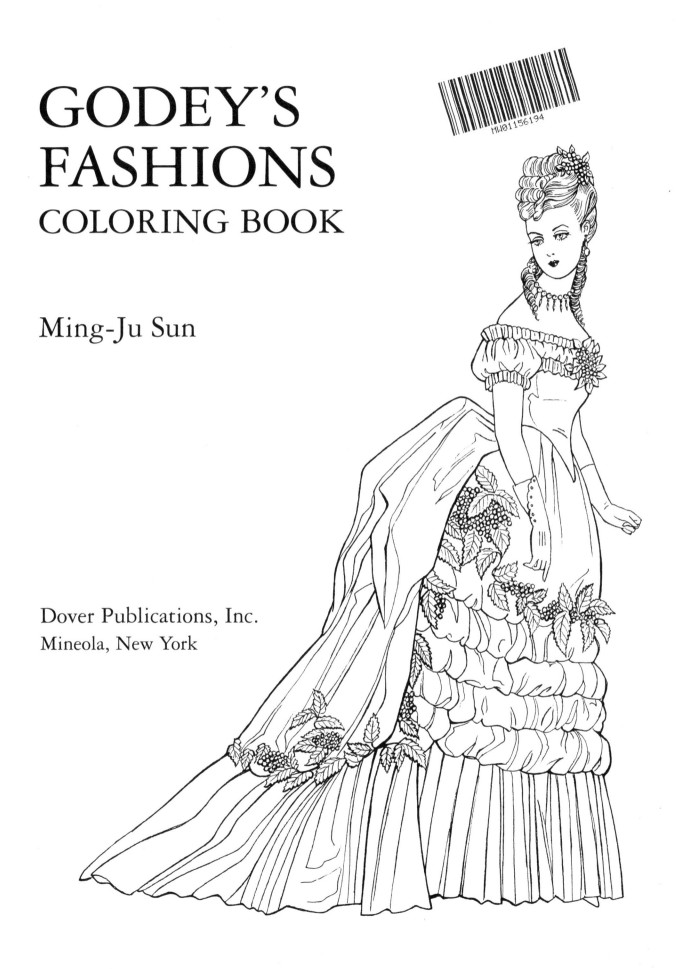

Dover Publications, Inc.
Mineola, New York

Publisher's Note

American women were treated to a new monthly magazine in 1830: the *Lady's Book* (later *Godey's Lady's Book*), published by Louis A. Godey in Philadelphia. Originally a literary publication offering serials, short stories, poems, and book reviews, the magazine was broadened to include fashions in the late 1830s. Under the editorial guidance of Sarah Josepha Hale, beginning in 1837, *Godey's Lady's Book* began to include fashion plates in color. The plates were based on foreign styles, especially those from Paris and Victorian England. Hale's contribution to the magazine went beyond fashion, however—as editor, she took advantage of the opportunity to address social injustices and promote the importance of women's education. Nevertheless, fashions and dress and needlework patterns were extremely popular with readers. The magazine's success was challenged by the arrival of publications such as *Harper's Bazar* (later *Bazaar*), founded in 1867, and the *Ladies' Home Journal* (1883). *Godey's* lasted until the end of the nineteenth century, ceasing publication in 1898.

The fashions that appear in this coloring book were depicted in *Godey's Lady's Book* between the years 1838 and 1880. As mentioned, the plates were derivative of Parisian and English fashions of the time: a model on page 2 wears a silk "Victoria"—a reference to the bonnet popular in Victorian England—and the model on page 10 shows off a French dress known as "La mathilde." From a dress with a "bertha" collar of English point lace to one with a *corsage à point* (pointed bodice), the delightful array of women's (and children's) fashions from *Godey's Lady's Book* offers a glimpse into the styles that delighted nineteenth-century American women.

Bibliographical Note

Godey's Fashions Coloring Book is a new work, first published by Dover Publications, Inc., in 2005.

International Standard Book Number

ISBN-13: 978-0-486-43998-3
ISBN-10: 0-486-43998-4

Manufactured in the United States by RR Donnelley
43998412   2015
www.doverpublications.com

1842. **Left:** This satin dress features three rows of puffing from shoulder to waist. The full sleeves have lace-edged shirring at the upper arm and the wrist; the V-neck bodice is lace-trimmed as well. **Right:** The form-fitting bodice has contrasting trim repeated in the multi-tiered skirt. Each tier has three layers of tucks. A lace insert can be seen in the deep V of the neckline.

1848. **Left:** The silk walking dress is paired with a *mantelet* (short cape) that is lavishly trimmed with lace. The lace edges the two broad panels at the front of the mantelet. **Right:** Two deep flounces define the wide skirt of this silk dress. A simple collar with a patterned cravat tops the dress's bodice. The model wears a patterned silk shawl over the dress.

1852. **Left:** The bodice of this mousseline housedress has an unusual criss-crossed drape, gathered at the shoulders and with a double layer of fabric edging (the sleeves have this edging as well). The deep V of the bodice leads into an apron with ruched edging on its sides and pockets. **Right:** This silk carriage dress has a tapering lace collar and broad lace decorations on the sleeves. Beneath the collar is a contrasting lace insert.

1855. **Left:** This organdy walking dress has a full skirt consisting of zig-zag–trimmed gathered layers. The dress front has a simple placket edged with lace. The collar and sleeves have more dramatic lace edging. The model wears a multi-tiered Spanish lace mantilla, which adds to the drama of the dress. **Right:** The model wears a taffeta walking dress that has satin ribbon "quilling" detail on the fitted jacket and skirt layers. Simple bows decorate the bodice front.

1855. **Left:** The extremely wide skirt of this silk walking dress owes its shape to a *pannier,* a framework of wire or other stiff material. The skirt's double layers are trimmed with stitched pleats; the pleats also appear at the edges of the puffed, gathered sleeves. The jacket closes by means of ribbon bows. Maltese lace adorns the collar and cuffs. **Right:** The skirt of this organdy dinner or walking dress is embellished with three bands of an intricate embroidered floral pattern. The model wears a lace mantelet trimmed with ribbon.

1860. This dress, known as "La mathilde," is worn with a scalloped- and embroidered-edged cape. The neckline has a double row of ruching. The voluminous dress flows from beneath the cape. The model wears a delicate lace wristband. Her large straw hat is trimmed with floral ornaments and broad ribbons.

1865. **Left:** The model's silk dress has a tunic skirt that is trimmed with a thick fringe. Her sleeves have ruching at the upper and lower edges. A long placket runs down the center of the tunic. The hemline of the full skirt is edged with ribbon. **Center:** The boy wears a light-gray suit that has buttons down the front of the tunic-styled jacket, as well as down the side of the short trousers. He wears tasseled boots and carries a straw hat decorated with black ribbon. **Right:** This poplinette dress is trimmed with thick chenille cord and has a modest lace collar.

1869. **Left:** The first of this trio of dresses is a velveteen walking suit with fringe-edged skirts. Large bows accent the dress. **Center:** This Watteau-styled evening dress derives its name from a dress style used by Watteau in his paintings—it is typified by a low neckline and loosely gathered pleats hanging from the shoulders in the back. Sprays of roses charmingly decorate the dress. **Right:** The upper skirt of this silk walking dress is looped up with a bow. An embroidered lace headpiece spills out onto the front of the costume.

14

1869. **Left:** This silk poplin walking dress has a velvet overdress. Beneath the draped apron is a skirt edged with scalloped lace; a long pleated skirt can be seen beneath that skirt. The dress's bodice has a strip of gathering from the shoulders through the bust. **Center:** The model wears a silk dinner dress whose skirt consists of gathered layers trimmed with satin and rosettes. The sleeves are gathered and puffed from shoulder to wrist. The bodice top has a panel of gathered rows. **Right:** The silk poplin housedress has broad bands of lace; rosettes are used to fasten the gathered skirts. At the back of the dress is a large bow, fastened by a narrow belt.

1872. **Left:** The model's silk grenadine (a fine-mesh fabric well-suited to warm weather) evening costume is embroidered with bird and flower motifs. The wide sleeves are edged with wide stitched pleats. The full skirt is accented with rows of eyelet embroidered lace. **Right:** This silk dinner dress is lavishly trimmed with silk ribbons, ruffles, and lace. Tiny buttons accent the elongated bodice. The skirt, made of narrow rows of gathered fabric, is framed by a lace-edged sideskirt.

1873. **Left:** A silk visiting costume is set off by the long button-trimmed lapels of the jacket. The oversized cuffs have the same button trim. Pleated silk edging trims the jacket. A tunic, which can be seen beneath the jacket, has a long fringe. Large bows and ribbons accent the layered skirt.

Right: The model's evening dress is embellished with silk ribbons on the bodice, sleeves, and skirt. The large skirt pouf is tied with an enormous bow that trails down the side. Large shirred ruffles encircle the skirt.

1874. **Left:** This off-the-shoulder evening dress is trimmed with rich Valenciennes lace, flowers, puffs, and embroidered muslin. Epaulet roses define the shoulders. **Center:** The overskirt of this silk evening dress is trimmed with scalloped lace. A modest lace shawl encircles the model's neck, fastened by a rose. The sleeves are trimmed with the same lace edging as the shawl. **Right:** Roses and leaves decorate the neckline and skirt of this silk evening dress. The skirt is given shape by a bustle. The model wears a cameo necklace.

1876. **Left:** This silk plaid walking dress has an overskirt that is trimmed with ribbons and gathered pleats. Ribbon-trimmed plaid swathes hang from the pouf at the back. The model wears a form-fitting vest decorated with a bow. A ribbon-trimmed purse hangs from the waistband. **Center:** The silk dinner dress features an overskirt of black lace, trimmed with gathered pleats and bows. The model's hair is decorated with matching black lace. The bodice ends in gathered pleats and lace. **Right:** French muslin plaiting trims this silk evening dress. Ruffles are looped into the pouf at the back. The silk is gathered in rows in the skirt.

1876. **Left:** The bodice and skirt of this silk walking dress are trimmed with plaid grenadine. Large bows decorate the front of the dress. The sleeves end in gathered, lace-trimmed pleats. **Center:** This silk bridal gown is trimmed with tasseled fringe and garlands of orange blossoms. Puffs of illusion appear from the waist to the hem. Elaborate lace-trimmed cuffs decorate the sleeves, topped with bows. A sheer veil trails to the floor. **Right:** A *matelassé* (heavyweight textile fabric) and silk visiting dress features large side buttons. The lapels and cuffs are made of a patterned cloth. Eyelet lace edges the neckline, and the cuffs end in gathered pleats.

1878. **Left:** This visiting dress, made of velvet and damask, is trimmed with lace, piping, and tasseled fringe. The dress has an overall embroidered pattern. Large buttons run down the dress front. **Center:** The model wears a silk grenadine dinner dress, trimmed with ecru lace, ribbons, and bows. **Right:** This silk evening dress is trimmed with Valenciennes lace and ribbon piping. The crossover front is lined with buttons, and buttons appear on the horizontal panels of the lower skirt as well.

1879. **Left:** The model's floral brocade evening dress has lace ruffles cascading from the neckline down to the lower skirt. Lace ruffles edge the plunging square neckline as well. The dress has an overall floral pattern. Bows decorate the sleeves and the gathered-up skirt. **Center:** The boy's velvet suit includes a cotton shirt trimmed with lace at the neck and cuffs. **Right:** This walking dress of silk brocade is trimmed with silk ribbon piping, pleated silk bands around the skirt, and bows at the wrist and along the sides of the skirt. It is interesting to note that the hairpiece incorporates an artificial bird.